Turn over a new leaf

'You'll have to excuse Gerald – it's the greenhouse effect.'

Turn over a new leaf

Green Cartoons for CARE

Edited by Mark Bryant

Earthscan Publications
London

First published in Great Britain 1990 by
Earthscan Publications Ltd
3 Endsleigh St
London WC1H 0DD

British Library Cataloguing in Publication Data
Turn over a new leaf
  1. International humorous cartoons
  I. Bryant, Mark
  741.5942

ISBN: 1-85383-085-2

Design by Mick Keates (071-381 6853)
Production by David Williams Associates (081-521 4130)
Typeset by Concise Graphics Ltd (071- 385 1411)
Printed and bound by Longdunn Printers Limited, Bristol

Earthscan Publications Ltd is a wholly owned and editorially
independent subsidiary of The International Institute for
Environment and Development (IIED).

PREFACE

All the cartoons in this book were originally donated for a fundraising auction and exhibition mounted by CARE Britain in 1990. Proceeds from the auction and all royalties from the continuing sale of this book will be donated to CARE to help their tree-planting, conservation and aid programmes worldwide.

Thanks are due to all the cartoonists whose generosity has made this book possible – despite the vagaries of the international postal system – and to the editors of the various newspapers and magazines in which some of the cartoons first appeared. More than 170 cartoons were donated by over 50 artists, many being drawn specially and in full colour, and submissions arrived from all over the world, irrespective of political regime or national boundaries.

Countries represented include Australia, Austria, Cuba, Cyprus, Czechoslovakia, France, Great Britain, Hungary, India, Ireland, Japan, Kenya, Lithuania, Mexico, New Zealand, Poland, Saudi Arabia, South Africa, Switzerland, USA and the USSR – proving that concern for the environment is indeed truly global.

Special thanks also go to all who have helped in the preparation of this book, in particular Julian Hopkins, Richard Cox, Frances Carroll, Anna Burland, Marie-Hélène Osterweil and Sally Austin at CARE Britain, and to Margaret Busby, Neil Middleton, Lavinia Greenlaw and Sian Mills at Earthscan Publications.

M.B.

ACKNOWLEDGEMENTS

For their kind permission to use the cartoons
in this book, CARE Britain and the publishers
would like to thank the following:

The Age (Melbourne)
Architects Journal
Le Canard Enchaîné
Daily News (Durban)
Dedeté
Frankfurter Allgemeine
Guardian
The Hindu
Independent Magazine
John Brown Publishing/House of Viz
Krokodil
Los Angeles Times
Ludas Matyi
Mirror Group Newspapers
Nebelspalter
Newsday
Private Eye
Punch
Radio Times
Riyadh Daily
Saudi Gazette
Stern
Sun (Melbourne)
Washington Post

Also Roger Woddis and *Radio Times* for the
use of 'Keep it Green'.

Keep It Green

The trouble with the human race,
Which wears a smirk upon its face
To indicate its massive mind,
Is being dumb and deaf and blind.

It does not hear the warning bell
To all that on this planet dwell,
It cannot see beyond this week,
It has a tongue, but does not speak.

The forest dies deprived of rain,
Lead damages the childish brain,
Pollution poisons turf and tide
And makes for global suicide.

We court disasters and disease,
And if, brought on by CFCs,
The Big Heat doesn't make us ill,
Be sure untreated water will.

The smallest creature in the wild,
The dinosaur that rarely smiled
And roamed the earth when life began
Is nowhere near as dumb as Man.

Roger Woddis

FOREWORD

Our world is threatened by an environmental crisis. Thirty-five acres of tropical forest are destroyed every minute and every fifteen seconds a species of flora or fauna becomes extinct. Pollution pervades our water supplies and the very air that we breathe.

This cartoon book has two aims. To make you smile and to make you think. Cartoonists from all over the world have contributed to this international anthology of environmental capers. The proceeds from its sale will go towards CARE's vital work with the world's poorest people in Africa, Asia and Latin America.

In the last decade CARE's environmental projects have planted 130 million trees and introduced soil-conservation techniques to thousands of farmers.

CARE recognizes the importance of trees to people living in the Third World. In Africa, for example, 90 per cent of the population rely on trees for fuel, fodder, food and shade.

I've been lucky enough to visit many of the world's countries and have seen for myself the importance of a healthy, safe environment. Looking after our planet is everybody's concern whether we live in Britain or Bangladesh, San Francisco or the Sudan.

I hope you'll enjoy *Turn Over A New Leaf*, which has been thoughtfully put together by CARE Britain. It represents a challenge to us all as we try to restock the earth's natural resources.

'At least we don't have to worry about *men* destroying our
environment!'

After a long, tough week landscaping in the hot sun —
Ernie ponders the significance of the greenhouse effect.

'Woke up this mornin' – got the Green Blues!'

'Whilst I would agree with you, madam, that we in the West must take
drastic steps to reduce consumption of fossil fuels – '

'Are you part of nature's delicate harmonious balance or just another
bloody weed?'

'We would have plenty of topsoil – but your bloody helicopters keep
blowing it away!'

LES BARTON

Catch of the day

'The greenhouse effect is very pronounced up here!'

'Someday they'll replace all that with a handful of computers and a
mile or two of electronic circuitry. But they'll *never* produce these
radioactive tomatoes, that acid rain, those sulphurous cabbages.'

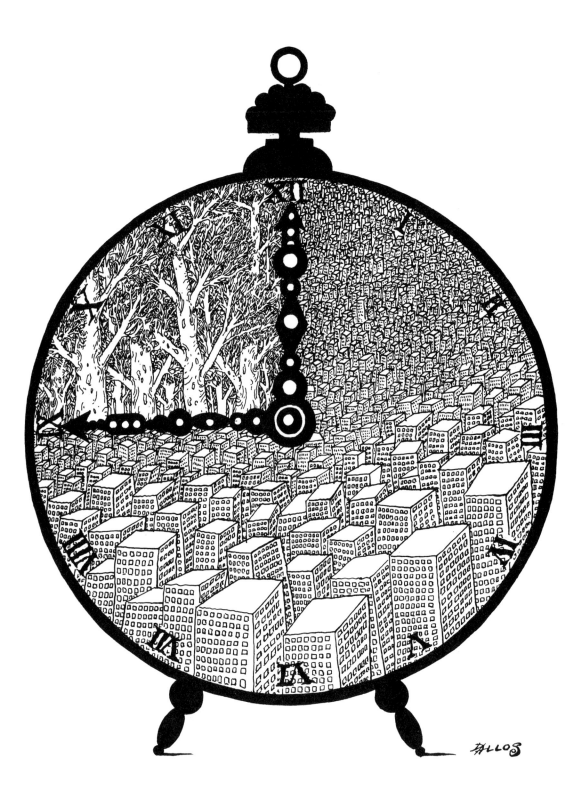

'And where would you get the wood pulp to manufacture the
newsprint for your complaints about de-forestation?'

'Is it unleaded?'

'We'll fell the trees to dig a mine, then flood the hole for
hydro–electricity!'

'Ah yes, just look how nice it is where we haven't been!'

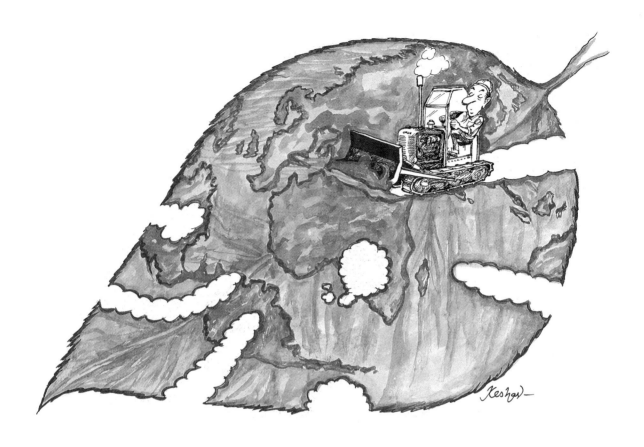

'And you think you've got problems!'

48

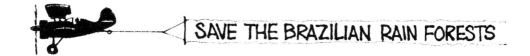

'Meanwhile, back in the Pacific north-west . . .'

'Like you, I feel we've got the policy just about right, but still have some
difficulty getting our message across to the people.'

1/8   S. BARNEKIS 89.

SOIL CONSERVATION AND TREE PLANTING STRATEGIES

'If God had wanted us to survive, he would have given us legs.'

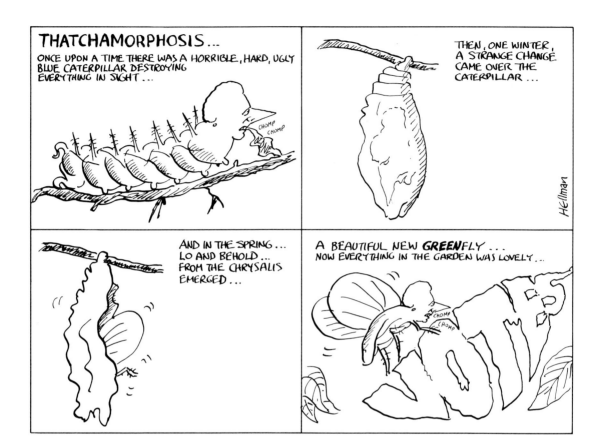

The disposable society

'That's not a square-ended plug, is it?'

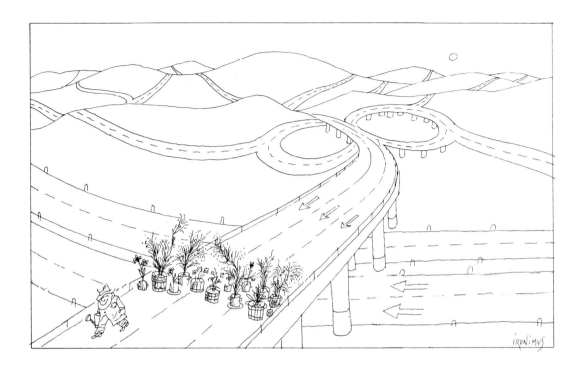

'If I were you, I'd take a torch as well.'

Patented waste–disposal unit

(The label on the Third World figure's arm reads: 'Member of the Basel
Convention on Toxic Waste' *Ed.*)

'I'm really looking forward to another experiment in our region.'

WHAT FUTURE ?

© MICHAEL ALANDO 1990

The warning voices of Nairobi

(The sign reads: 'We are all very concerned!!! *Ed.*)

OZONE

Abdurahim ALireza
JEDDAH, SAUDI ARABIA
NOVEMBER 1989

'I think that I shall never see a poem lovely as decree.'

'It's everywhere, mindless bloody graffiti . . .'

'The future is not going to judge us by how much megawatt energy we
produce or how many super-highways we've constructed, but rather by
how much nature we've left behind for our children.'

INDEX OF CARTOONS

CONTRIBUTING CARTOONISTS

ABDURAHIM ALIREZA *Saudi Arabia*

Abdurahim Alireza was born in 1925 in Jeddah, Saudi Arabia, and was encouraged to draw on paper at an early age when his parents became exasperated by the grotesque graffiti with which he covered the walls of their home. After a number of years working as a cartoonist and illustrator for an oil magazine he joined the *Saudi Gazette* (1976-80), then moved to *Arab News* (1982-6) before returning to the *Gazette* in 1988.

MIROSLAV BARTAK *Czechoslovakia*

Born in 1938 'partly by mistake and partly by the wish of my parents', Miroslav Bartak spent ten years as an engineer in the merchant navy before realizing – at the age of 30 – that it was high time he started doing something for real. So he stayed at home in Prague and started drawing and painting, which he has been doing ever since.

LES BARTON *UK*

Having had no formal training as an artist, Les Barton became a cartoonist – which qualified him as a retouching artist for photographs of cars, cans and cattle. He then worked in advertising and comics ('Billy Bunter', 'I Spy' and 'Harry's Haunted House') and now draws mainly for *Punch* and *Private Eye* when not designing humorous greetings cards. He is also Treasurer of the Cartoonists' Club of Great Britain.

JIM BERRY *USA*

Born in Chicago, Jim Berry graduated in business administration from Ohio Wesleyan University and joined the US Navy's Famous Artists Cartoon Course before working in a wide variety of animation projects for TV commercials. In 1963, after joining the art department of the Newspaper Enterprise Association, he created 'Berry's World', now the most widely syndicated editorial cartoon feature in the USA. A past president of the Association of American Editorial Cartoonists, Jim Berry has five times won National Cartoonists Society awards, as well as receiving numerous other prizes for his work. The author of *Life in the Mall Lane*, he is married with two grown-up sons and divides his year between homes in Florida and Cape Cod.

RUPERT BESLEY *UK*

Born in Norfolk in 1950 and now living on the Isle of Wight, Rupert Besley taught for several years before moving into full-time cartoon work. Dealing mainly in book illustrations and designs for greetings cards and postcards, his work has also appeared in a variety of publications, including *Punch*, *Private Eye*, *New Statesman* and *Times Educational Supplement*.

'BIFF' (Chris Garratt & Mick Kidd) *UK*

The two artists who comprise Biff Products met at school in Leicestershire in the 1950s and have been collaborating on comic projects of one sort or another ever since. Mick Kidd is a history graduate of Swansea University and now lives in London, working as a writer and operating a Biff Products stall in Camden Lock market. Chris Garratt took a degree in Fine Art at the Bath Academy of Art and lives in Devon with his wife and three children. He is also a lecturer and film-maker. Biff Products began in the 1970s with a range of lapel buttons and postcards and occasional contributions to such 'alternative' newspapers as *International Times*. Biff cartoons now appear regularly in *City Limits* and the *Guardian* and five collections have been published, with a sixth, *BIFF's Bonanza*, in preparation. A touring exhibition of originals is available from the Watershed Media Centre, Bristol.

'CARLUCHO' (Carlos Villar Aleman) *Cuba*

Carlucho was born in Matanzas, Cuba, in 1946 and is the director of DDT, an association of Cuban cartoonists based in Havana which produces a fortnightly satirical broadsheet, *Dedeté*, full of wry comments on politics and people, both in Cuba and abroad. Carlucho's work has been exhibited and published in Cuba, Canada, Poland, Mexico, Belgium, Turkey, Italy, USSR, USA, UK, Bulgaria, Yugoslavia, Japan, Nicaragua and Greece and he has won 15 international awards, including a number of gold medals.

'CHAS' (Chas Sinclair) *UK*

Chas Sinclair left school at 14 and began work in the aircraft industry before leaving to draw editorial cartoons for the *TV Post*. After a period working as a designer for a linen manufacturer he was made redundant in 1967 and has been a freelance cartoonist ever since, contributing to the *Mail on Sunday, Shoot!* etc.

PAUL CONRAD   *USA*

Educated at the University of Iowa, Paul Conrad was editorial cartoonist at the *Denver Post* from 1950 to 1963 and joined the *Los Angeles Times*, where he remains today, in 1964. Four collections of his cartoons have been published and examples of his work (including bronze sculptures) have been exhibited in the Los Angeles Museum of Art. Paul Conrad's cartoons have regularly carried off some of the most prestigious awards in the business, including three Pulitzer Prizes (1964, 1971 and 1984), and he has won the distinguished service award of the US National Society of Professional Journalists no less than six times. He is married with four children.

TOM DARCY   *USA*

Tom Darcy was born in Brooklyn, New York, in 1932 and served in the US Navy during the Korean War before studying art at the School of Visual Arts in New York, where he received the Outstanding Graduate Award. He joined *Newsday* as editorial cartoonist in 1959 and then moved to the *Houston Post* and *Philadelphia Bulletin* before returning to *Newsday* in 1968, where he remains today. He has won numerous prestigious national and international awards for his work, including a Pulitzer Prize in 1970 and the Grand Prize of the United Nations in 1975, for his penetrating and compassionate cartoons on the crisis of world famine. Tom Darcy lives in North Bellmore, Long Island, with his wife and four children.

ALAN DE LA NOUGEREDE   *UK*

Born in Nowgong, India, Alan de la Nougerede was a professional accountant in the City and the provinces before becoming a full-time artist/cartoonist. His first cartoon for *Punch* appeared in 1970 and he is now widely published in the UK and USA. He has produced strip cartoons for the *Daily Express, Evening News* and *Post* and was Editorial Cartoonist of the *People* 1986-8. His watercolours have been exhibited in Ebury St and Bayswater Rd, London. He is married with one daughter.

'DISH' (Neil Dishington)   *UK*

Born: a long time ago. Art school, teaching, illustrations, cartooning, mending the fence, bringing up children etc.

Now over 50 but, like Tomi Ungerer, believes that all he has done is 'merely an apprenticeship for what is to follow'.

SIMON DONALD   *UK*

'When I was little I went to school. And then I grew up. Later I did cartoons. Cartoons are what I do now. I have got a flat and two cars. Both my cars are red. But both of them are not the same red as each other. I am not married and all the girls I go out with chuck me. Sometimes I go out with girls and I chuck them.' (One of *Viz* magazine's contributing cartoonists, Simon Donald acknowledges a debt to Graham Dury and Simon Thorp for additional material used in the drawing published in this book. *Ed.*)

STAN EALES   *UK*

Born in New Zealand in 1962, Stan Eales currently lives in London and is a graphic designer by day and a cartoonist after hours. A regular contributor to *Green Magazine* and an irregular one to *Punch* and *Private Eye,* he was green long before it became *à la mode.* Married with no sproglets (yet), his star sign is Cancer.

HORST HAITZINGER   *West Germany*

Born in Eferding, Austria, in 1939, Horst Haitzinger studied commercial art in Linz for four years before moving to Munich to study painting and graphics. His first political caricature appeared in *Simplicissimus* in 1958 and he has been a regular contributor to the magazine ever since. He has also had cartoons and illustrations published in a wide variety of newspapers and journals in Germany, Austria and Switzerland and his drawings and oil paintings ('Fantastic Realism') have frequently been exhibited both in Germany and elsewhere. He lives and works in Munich.

WALTER HANEL   *West Germany*

Born in 1930 in Teplitz-Schönau in Czechoslovakia, Walter Hanel has contributed to various newspapers and magazines since 1958, notably *Pardon, Simplicissimus* and *Kölner Stadtanzeiger*. Since 1981 he has been political cartoonist on the *Frankfurter Allgemeine* and has received a number of honours for his work, including the Thomas Nast Prize and the Wilhelm Busch Prize. He has also worked on radio, published books of his cartoons and had his drawings exhibited in Germany and abroad. He lives with his wife and daughter in Bergisch Gladbach near Cologne.

LOUIS HELLMAN   *UK*

Born in London in 1936, Louis Hellman studied architecture at universities in London and Paris (B. Arch 1962) and now works as an architect/designer/illustrator. He has been cartoonist for the *Architects Journal* since 1967 and his work has also appeared in *Architectural Review, Building Design, Observer, Sunday Times, New Statesman* etc. He produced an animated cartoon film for BBC2 in 1974 and there was an exhibition of his work at the Architectural Association in 1979. Louis Hellman has published three books (including *Architecture for Beginners*, 1986), and has lectured widely in the UK, USA, Australia and Singapore.

'HERBLOCK' (Herbert Block)   *USA*

Born and educated in Chicago, Herblock was editorial cartoonist for the *Chicago Daily News* and NEA Service before joining the *Washington Post* in 1946. He has won numerous prestigious awards for his work including Pulitzer Prizes in 1942, 1954 and 1979 and is the only living cartoonist to have his work exhibited in the US National Gallery of Art. He has had honorary degrees conferred on him by no less than six US universities and colleges, is a fellow of the American Academy of Arts and Sciences and his work is syndicated to 300 newspapers worldwide. Ten collections of his cartoons have appeared to date and he has also designed postage stamps.

'IRONIMUS' (Gustav Peichl)   *Austria*

Born in Vienna in 1928, Gustav Peichl studied architecture at the Vienna Academy of Fine Art and became Professor of Architecture there in 1973. He has designed numerous public buildings which have won international acclaim and is the author of several books. This distinguished architect's second career, as a cartoonist, began in 1955 and he is a regular contributor to *Die Presse, Suddeutsche Zeitung* and *Die Wochenpresse*.

'JEFF' (Geoffrey Hook)   *Australia*

Born in Hobart, Tasmania, in 1928, Jeff worked on the Hobart *Mercury* until 1964 before joining the Melbourne *Sun* where he has worked ever since. He has written and illustrated books for children and won many awards for his work both in Australia and overseas.

DALLOS JENÖ   *Hungary*

After school Dallos Jenö worked in a mine before beginning his National Service in 1960. He later became a graphic artist for the Hungarian National Institute of Medical Films and joined the staff of the satirical magazine *Ludas Matyi* in 1970. A member of the Hungarian National Association of Fine Arts, he has had 13 books of his work published, won numerous awards, produced three animated films and designed stamps for the Hungarian postal service. His cartoons have appeared in a variety of international journals including *Punch, Das Magazin* and *Pardon*.

'KESHAV'   *India*

Five years of social cartooning in the regional language weekly, *Ananda Vikatan*, gave Keshav the confidence to quit banking (he has a postgraduate qualification in commerce) and join *The Hindu* where he has been staff cartoonist for the past 2½ years. He also works as a caricaturist and illustrator.

KROKODIL   *USSR*

Krokodil was first published in Moscow in 1922 as the humour supplement to the weekly *Workers' Journal (Rabochaia gazeta)*. Under its founding editor, K.S. Eremeev, it quickly rose to fame for its satirical writing and the cartoons of such eminent artists as Boris Efimov, the Kukryniksi group and Deni. It has been an independent publication since 1932 and now appears three times a month. The cartoons featured in this book are by V. Vladov, V. Dmitriuk and R. Drukman.

DAVID LANGDON OBE   *UK*

An ex-RAF squadron leader, David Langdon is a regular contributor to *Punch, New Yorker* and other publications and is a member of the *Punch* 'Table'. He has also illustrated books, including a series of humorous titles by George Mikes, and is official artist to the Centre Internationale Audio-Visuel. He is married with three children and lives in Buckinghamshire.

JOCK LEYDEN   *South Africa*

Born on 21 November 1908 in Grangemouth, Scotland, Jock Leyden was educated in Glasgow and studied art in Durban and London (Hetherleys and Central London schools) before working as a freelance artist and illustrator. He was political cartoonist on the Durban *Sunday Tribune* from 1937 to 1972 and joined the Durban *Daily News* in 1939. He has had 14 books of his cartoons published and has received many awards and honours including South

African Cartoonist of the Year (1982), the Papal Cross (1987) and Durban Civic Honours (1989). He is married with a son and three daughters.

TIMOTHY LINDSEY *Australia*

Timothy Lindsey is a Melbourne artist and cartoonist whose work appears regularly in the Melbourne *Age* and *Herald* newspapers. He has also illustrated a number of books.

'MARKUS' (Joerg von Morgen) *West Germany*

An account executive in an advertising agency before joining *Stern* magazine as cartoonist, Markus has published seven books of his work to date. He also plays baritone saxophone in a jazz band and enjoys the novels of Trollope and P.G. Wodehouse. Married with three children, Markus lives in Hamburg.

'MOLLUSC' (Brian West) *UK*

Better known by his pen-name, 'Mollusc', Brian West became a full-time writer and cartoonist in 1982 after ten years working in television. His cartoon strip 'Newshound' is syndicated to newspapers all over Britain. From his London studio, the Cartoon Factory, he also writes scripts for IPC Comics' versions of such legendary characters as Woody Woodpecker and Scooby Doo.

HANS MOSER *Switzerland*

Born in Switzerland in 1922, Hans Moser emigrated to the USA in 1927 and served in the US Army during the Second World War. He studied graphic arts in New York, Paris and Lausanne and was political cartoonist for a Danish newspaper in Copenhagen from 1953 to 1963, when he moved to Laax in the Swiss Alps. He has been a regular contributor to *Nebelspalter* since 1954 (in which he also has a weekly column) and in addition writes short stories. He has had 11 collections of his work published and has won a number of awards.

SERGIO NAVARRO *Mexico/UK*

Sergio Navarro, who comes from Culiacan in the north of Mexico, is equally well known for his drawing, murals and cartoons. Since arriving in London eight years ago he has taught visual arts and graphics, produced cartoons and illustrations for a variety of books and magazines – including *Punch* – created three murals and designed publicity material for the tenth anniversary of the Nicaraguan Revolution. His work has been exhibited at a number of galleries in London and Mexico.

DAVIDSON NJOROGE *Kenya*

Born on 21 February 1963 in the Nyeri district of Kenya, Davidson Njoroge studied graphic design and communication and worked in a number of advertising agencies before joining CARE International. He now works as Production Manager in Development Graphics and Design for CARE's East Africa Regional Advisory Team.

'PEACOCK' (Oliver Hacker) *West Germany*

The second of three children, Oliver Hacker was born in Munich and studied graphic design before joining an advertising agency in 1987. Since 1988 he has been working as a freelance graphic designer, illustrator and cartoonist based in Munich.

GRAHAM PHILPOT *UK*

Graham Philpot was born on 26 May 1955 in Ipswich, Suffolk, and works as a freelance illustrator, specializing in the advertising, design and editorial fields. Recent commissions have included London Transport posters, Paperchase designs and various regular items for *The Times* and *Radio Times*. He has also illustrated children's books for Collins and Conran Octopus/Mothercare and was a prizewinner in the 1986 Benson & Hedges 'Style' Competition. He is married with three children and lives in Acton, London.

PIED CROW *Kenya*

Pied Crow was founded by CARE in association with the Kenyan Ministry of Education in July 1983 as a teaching aid for Kenyan primary schools. At present 15,000 schools receive copies of the magazine which treats subjects such as natural-resource conservation, health, population and practical skills in full-colour comic-strip form. More than 1,352,000 copies and over 30 issues have been printed since its inception. The magazine, whose full title is *Pied Crow's Environment Special Magazine*, is completely drawn, designed, printed and packaged in Kenya and uses the work of local illustrators such as Davidson Njoroge and Michael Alando.

RAJINDER PURI *India*

Cartoonist, editorial writer, political columnist, satirist and activist, Rajinder Puri is no stranger to controversy.

Whether leading 3000 *jhuggi*-dwellers in a demonstration or provoking the ire of 25 MPs for his inflammatory cartoon work, Puri's commitment to his beliefs is total. A postgraduate in history from Delhi University, he began his career as a newspaper cartoonist for such publications as the *Guardian* and *Glasgow Herald* in the UK and *Hindustan Times* and the *Statesman* in India. He has been freelance since 1970 and has written two books on Indian politics as well as founding three political parties. He lives in Delhi.

KEN PYNE   *UK*

Started off as a layout artist on *Scrap* and *Waste Reclamation and Disposal Weekly* before turning freelance, since when he's been taken up by *The Times*, *Private Eye*, *Punch*, *Observer*, *Independent Magazine* and others.

BRYAN READING   *UK*

Bryan Reading was roughed out in 1935 and after too many years in advertising became a full-time inker in 1978. The colours may have faded a bit, but the general outline remains. He works for all the usual cartoon markets.

TONY REEVE   *UK*

Born 1961. Showed early concern for the environment by demanding unbleached nappies. Became an eco-cartoonist (recycled jokes in lead-free pencil) in 1986. Work has appeared in *Private Eye*, *Spectator*, *Punch* and *The Damage*.

ARTHUR REID   *UK*

An international freelance cartoonist, illustrator and sculptor, ARThur (*sic*) Reid was educated at Aberdeen College of Commerce, Gray's School of Art and Aberdeen College of Education. His work has appeared in *Punch*, *Private Eye*, *Playboy* and *Penthouse* and has been exhibited worldwide, earning him numerous medals and awards including being the first-ever British prizewinner of the World Cartoon Exhibition in Belgium in 1980. He is also the organizer of the Edinburgh International Cartoon Festival and is employed as a part-time art specialist by Grampian Regional Council. He lives and sometimes works in Scotland and lists his hobbies as beer and collecting 'first edition' rejection slips.

SAM SMITH   *UK*

A freelance cartoonist and illustrator whose work appears in *The Times*, *Independent* and various magazines and journals, Sam Smith wages a constant war with editors who have no sense of humour and even less taste. A freelance for the last 15 years, he would like to return in his next life as a commissioning editor with total power over editors with no sense of humour.

REG SMYTHE   *UK*

Reg Smythe was born and still lives in Hartlepool. He started cartooning in 1954 and created 'Andy Capp' for the *Daily Mirror* in 1957. The strip has been syndicated to 48 countries outside the UK, has been translated into 14 languages and currently appears in 1700 newspapers. Reg says that Andy might be a little devil but he's been very good to *him*.

DAVID STOTEN   *UK*

Born on 28 April 1962, David Stoten graduated in Graphic Design and Illustration from St Martin's School of Art. A regular contributor to *Mad* magazine, he began work at Spitting Image Productions in 1984 as assistant caricaturist, learning to sculpt under the watchful eyes of Roger Law and Peter Fluck. Since 1987 he has been senior caricaturist in charge of drawing and modelling for the studio, which produces caricature puppets for the immensely popular satirical TV show of the same name.

ALPER SUSUZLU   *Cyprus*

Alper Susuzlu was born in 1954 in the village of Suskhu, in the Paphos district of Cyprus, and studied art in Istanbul. A founder member of the Turkish Cypriot Cartoonists' Association, his cartoons and paintings have been exhibited widely and he has won a number of international awards. As well as art he also has a professional interest in the theatre, having founded the Turkish Cypriot Comedy Theatre and written three plays, and was president of the MET Cultural Association between 1979 and 1988. He is married with one son.

RON TANDBERG   *Australia*

One of Australia's best known and most honoured cartoon artists, Tandberg's front-page drawings are usually the first thing to take the reader's eye in the Melbourne *Age*, Sydney *Morning Herald* and *West Australian*. Though he started out as a teacher, he is now a master of cartoon irony and has had several collections of his cartoons published.

LES TANNER *Australia*

Les Tanner has been a cartoonist since 1944 and his warm wit regularly takes the features cartoon spot in the Melbourne *Age,* to which he also contributes a weekly humorous column every Saturday. He has worked for a number of papers in Australia and overseas, both as a cartoonist and a journalist, and has received two Walkley Awards for his work.

'TROG' (Wally Fawkes) *UK*

Born in Vancouver, Canada, in 1924 Wally Fawkes came to the UK in 1931 and has been cartooning since 1945. His work has been widely published in *Punch* and other journals and his well-known strip, 'Flook', ran for 35 years (1949–84) in the *Daily Mail.* He now works for the *Observer,* which he joined in 1965.

MARTYN TURNER *Ireland*

Martyn Turner has been the political cartoonist of the *Irish Times* since 1976 and also contributes a monthly cartoon to *New Internationalist.* A member of the Cartoonists' and Writers' Syndicate of New York, he has had five collections of his work published and is co-author of a book on political cartoons. He lives in the ecologically unspoilt Irish countryside surrounded by other people's litter.

MIKE TURNER *UK*

Mike Turner is 47 and has been cartooning since 1976. His work has appeared in many publications including *Reader's Digest, Private Eye, Spectator* and *Punch.* He was Hon. Secretary of the Cartoonists' Club of Great Britain for five years and lists his hobby as decoding British Rail timetables. He lives in Colchester.

'WOZNIAK' *France/Poland*

Born in Cracow, Poland, in 1954, Wozniak arrived in Paris in 1982 and contributed to such publications as *Libération, Playboy* and *L'Evénement du Jeudi* before working exclusively for the *Le Canard Enchaîné* (from 1987). His paintings have also been exhibited in Poland and the USA.

YASUO YOSHITOMI *Japan*

Born in Kyoto in 1938, Yasuo Yoshitomi studied graphic design at Kyoto Fine Art University and in 1973 set up the world's first cartoon and caricature department – of which he is professor – in the Faculty of Art at Kyoto Seika University. He was awarded the first Grand Prize of the Japanese Cartoonists' Association in 1970 and has produced animated cartoons for Japanese television. Elected to the committee of the Society of Japanese Cartoonists in 1982 he is also President of the Kyoto International Humorist Society.

MIKE YULE *New Zealand*

Mike Yule is a 26-year-old cartoonist working for the New Zealand *Listener* and a variety of environmental publications. He currently lives in Wellington developing the Great Malfunction Theory, which maintains that industrial capitalism is best likened to an addle-pated, blundering corpulent sot in a loud seersucker shirt which will very soon violently implode in one vast spontaneous, simultaneous maelstrom of malfunctioning appliances.

Note Biographical details of other contributors have been omitted at their own request (*Ed.*).

TRIBUTES TO THE WORK OF CARE

'In the hot dry conditions of Africa and India, dehydration is more than serious. It is a killer. Five million children die for lack of treatment every year . . . I am determined that we should do everything we can do to help. I very much hope you feel the same way, and will want to play your part in helping CARE.'

Julie Andrews

'The earth is in environmental crisis, nothing less. So I'm delighted to support CARE's crucial tree-planting programme. They've been in the field long enough to know that trees mean life . . . But we haven't got enough and we've lost far too many. So we're going to have to plant *millions* of them . . . I can't think of a more effective investment in a better world.'

David Bellamy

'Having spent many of my early years in India, I've seen something of the poverty that afflicts the Third World. CARE is one of the largest charities in the world, treating the sick and feeding millions of hungry people in the dozens of countries in which it works. That is why I support them.'

Felicity Kendal

'I welcome this opportunity to pay warm tribute to the extensive and noble work of CARE in securing the basic needs of so many people in the Third World. I am particularly pleased to see how CARE Britain has grown over the past few years. We look forward to continuing our support for its most valuable work and send our warm wishes to all those helping to achieve its important goals.'

Rt Hon. Margaret Thatcher MP

'If you can, please help CARE to help others.'

Glenda Jackson

'I congratulate all of the wonderful people who have dedicated their time, their efforts and, yes, their real care to the work of CARE ... Truly CARE is meeting the challenge. With the millions of people you have helped, I join in a resounding "thank you" ... and may God continue to bless you in your noble mission.'

Ronald Reagan

'Having travelled with CARE Britain's National Director, I was very impressed by CARE's long-term development projects in Africa. Band Aid supports them fully.'

Bob Geldof

'Please join me in contributing to CARE's vital work with the poor and needy millions throughout the developing world . . . helping to build a better future through self-help programmes.'

Jilly Cooper

Nikki English

'One of the reasons why I'm so keen on working with CARE, is that CARE is an organization which does face up to the challenges of becoming more managerially competent, with a great deal of honesty and integrity. Appraisal, design and evaluation of projects, all these things matter to CARE.'

Rt Hon. Christopher Patten MP

'The challenges facing many peoples of the world are to find the means to earn a basic livelihood, to feed and clothe their children, to have the chance for even a rudimentary education. The work of CARE Britain makes a valuable contribution to these efforts, for which the financial support of individuals and businesses is the key.'

Donald S. MacDonald, Canadian High Commissioner

'I am well aware of the work of CARE and of their efforts to help the underprivileged of the world and I support them fully. I wish CARE Britain well in all its activities.'

Douglas McClelland, Australian High Commissioner

During the last decade an estimated 130 million trees have been planted by CARE.

CARE was founded over 40 years ago to send food aid and relief to stricken British and other European families recovering from the devastation of the Second World War. Today it has grown into one of the world's largest and most effective international relief and development agencies, working in 38 countries and with particular concern for agroforestry, environmental conservation, irrigation, small-business support, education, training and primary health care in the developing world.

The environment has now become a major concern for everybody and CARE is proud to have been recognized for its leading contribution to environmental conservation over the last 20 years – particularly to reforestation in the Third World – by receiving the prestigious United Nations Environment Programme Global 500 award. In the last decade alone CARE has planted over 130 million trees and continues to plant at the rate of 32 million a year.

In addition, our investment in environmental education and training, agricultural improvements and erosion control – all under the direction of highly qualified foresters and agriculturalists – has allowed many hundreds of thousands of farmers throughout the developing world to make sustainable use of their environment rather than deplete its resources.

But with deforestation in South America, acid rain, crop diseases and pests, not to mention the devastating floods, droughts and hurricanes that we have all witnessed in recent times, there is still much to be done. And, as a registered charity our very existence depends on donations from the public to help us help others less fortunate and to put our aid programmes into practice.

If you would like to help support CARE in any way, however small, please contact CARE Britain's National Director, Julian Hopkins, at the address below or get in touch with the Director of any of the other national CARE offices listed overleaf.

Julian Hopkins, National Director, CARE Britain,
Dudley House, 36–38 Southampton Street, London WC2E 7HE
Tel: 071-379 5247.

CARE OFFICES WORLDWIDE

Australia
Ian Harris
National Director
CARE Australia
GPO Box 2014
Canberra 2601
AUSTRALIA

Austria
Dr Victor Beerman
National Director
CARE Austria
Wedertorgasse 15/1/16
1010 Vienna
AUSTRIA

Canada
Dr A.J. Watson
Executive Director
CARE Canada
BP/PO Box 9000
1550 Carling Avenue
Ottawa
Ontario K1G 4X6
CANADA

Denmark
Jan Kieler
National Director
CARE Denmark
Borgerade 14
PO Box 9058
DK-1022 Copenhagen K
DENMARK

France
National Director
CARE France
107 Rue de Longchamp
75116 Paris
FRANCE

Italy
National Director
CARE Italy
Via Raffaele Cadorna 29
00187 Rome
ITALY

Japan
Ambassador Yokota
National Director
CARE Japan
306 Hainesu Rowaiyaru
3-7-26 Nishishinjuku
Shinjuku-ku
Tokyo 160
JAPAN

Norway
Torkild Skallerud
National Director
CARE Norway
PO Box 8226
Hammersborg
1029 Olso 1
NORWAY

USA
Dr Phil Johnston
President
CARE USA
660 First Avenue
New York NY 10016
USA

West Germany
Janny Bahn
National Director
CARE West Germany
Wesselstrasse 12
5300 Bonn 1
WEST GERMANY